Henry Martyn Dexter

The Church Polity of the Pilgrims

The Polity of the New Testament

Henry Martyn Dexter

The Church Polity of the Pilgrims
The Polity of the New Testament

ISBN/EAN: 9783337292430

Printed in Europe, USA, Canada, Australia, Japan

Cover: Foto ©Lupo / pixelio.de

More available books at **www.hansebooks.com**

THE
CHURCH POLITY OF THE PILGRIMS

THE POLITY OF

THE NEW TESTAMENT.

BY

HENRY M. DEXTER.

WITH AN INTRODUCTION BY HON. R. A. CHAPMAN,
CHIEF JUSTICE OF THE SUPREME COURT OF MASSACHUSETTS.

BOSTON:
CONGREGATIONAL PUBLISHING SOCIETY.
1870.

[FIFTY COPIES PRINTED.]

INTRODUCTION.

Boston, June 30, 1870.

My Dear Sir, — When the articles containing the substance of this little work were first published in "The Congregationalist and Recorder," I read them with much interest, and expressed to you a hope that they might be re-published in a more permanent form. The practical importance of the subject of church government and polity appears to me to be vastly greater than many people seem to suppose. Congregational government is radically different from hierarchy in any of its forms. The former regards the members of a Christian church as capable of managing the affairs of the church: while the latter regards them as incompetent to manage those affairs; not capable of deciding upon the admission, discipline, or expulsion of their fellow-members, nor of maintaining fellowship with other churches. It, therefore, reduces them to the condition of a governed class; their duty being simply to obey the hierarchy, whose competency to govern them is assumed. You have shown which of these systems of government is in conformity with the teachings of the New Testament. And if we go farther back, and consider the fundamental object of Christianity, we are led to the same result. Christ's purpose manifestly was to renovate and elevate mankind by acting upon them individually. He taught the value of man as an individual; exposed the true character of the evil that is in him and tends to degrade him; and his plan of renovation begins with faith in himself personally, and proceeds with attachment and obedience to himself. The organization and observances which he prescribed to his followers were very simple; and as the preservation and propagation of his system were to be not by coercion, but, so far as man's agency is concerned, principally by teaching and example, very little of church government was needed, and that little could be managed by a local assembly. He regarded all men as brethren, and all of them erring and sinful; but the sin towards which he manifested a special detestation was the lust and abuse of official power.

The tendency of a hierarchy would naturally be adverse to his system; and knowing how strong the lust of power is in the human heart, and foreseeing its effects, we should naturally expect that he would give a solemn command, like that which he gave when he spoke of the exercise of lordship and authority by princes and great men among the Gentiles, and peremptorily declared, " So shall it not be among you." It was addressed to those who were to be the teachers and preachers of his system; and, had it been obeyed after the days of the apostles, the tendency would have been to purify and ennoble that class of his followers, by saving them from the degrading temptation to claim lordship and authority over their brethren.

Our ancestors came here fresh from the experience of hierarchal oppression and cruelty. Their ministers were learned men, and well acquainted with ecclesiastical history. They knew how early the lust of power began to operate upon Christian ministers, and how it grew till the prominent feature of ecclesiastical history, through all the intervening ages, had become a history of the oppression and degradation of the laity by the hierarchy. It is a frightful history for a layman to read.

Hierarchy had been a blight upon human liberty and progress, and upon Christianity itself. They knew that its authority rested upon tradition; and therefore they went behind tradition, to the New Testament itself. There they found, as you find, popular sovereignty; and, renouncing all claim to lordship and authority, they taught their brethren their rights and their duties in this respect. The introduction of this new system of government gave not only a new position, but naturally tended to give a new elevation of character, to the brethren. They were no longer mere subjects, living under the dictation of office-holders, but themselves possessed the rights of sovereignty. As the New Testament expresses it, they were "a royal priesthood," not subject to a human priest; "kings and priests unto God," having equal rights among themselves; and this is the very essence of a pure democracy.

Attached to the rights of this common sovereignty are its dignity, its responsibilities, and its duties; and a religious regard for them tends to elevate men towards their highest capabilities. It teaches them the need of universal education. Thus it originated the common school, which put education under the control of the people. It fits them for self government, and thus it led to the establishment of our civil government based on popular sovereignty. It is hostile to every form of monarchy and aristocracy, as tending to degrade the people. It lays the foundations of popular civil government in religious principle, and supplies restraints against wrong-doing, which human government is incapable of supplying, — the Bible being, in fact, the textbook of civil liberty. It trains the members of the church to the exercise of the rights of sovereignty, in the management of their business, in a Christian spirit of charity, forbearance, and deference to the opinions and feelings of others, instead of a spirit of wilfulness, conceit, and selfishness; a training which is of incalculable value to any citizen in a popular government. And it elevates the ministry to a higher class of duties than those belonging to dictation and coercion, and tends to purify and ennoble them.

It is not necessary to speak in commendation of its influence upon the character and destiny of this country. The Cambridge Platform, notwithstanding the defect noticed by you, preserved the essence of popular sovereignty, by leaving not only the choice of officers, but the admission, discipline, and expulsion of members, and maintaining fellowship with "neighbor churches," and, indeed, all the business of the church, in the hands of the people; but, unfortunately, in later times there arose, in the minds of some of the influential ministers, a want of confidence in the capacity of the people, and a desire for official authority and dictation; and this led to a neglect of instruction as to the duties of the people in maintaining self-government, and the spirit in which these duties should be discharged. Experience has shown that these men made a mistake, and I believe your discussion of the subject will do great good.

Yours very respectfully,
R. A. CHAPMAN.

REV. H. M. DEXTER, D.D.

THE CHURCH POLITY OF THE PILGRIMS

THE

POLITY OF THE NEW TESTAMENT.

The Plymouth Pilgrims were stigmatized as " Brownists ; " but the careful student of their actual belief and practice will more likely conclude, not only that they were Congregationalists, but that the current Congregationalism of the United States now reproduces much more exactly that which they held, and which John Robinson so ably expounded, than it does the not quite semi-Presbyterianism of Cotton's " Keyes," and of the " Cambridge Platform." In the matter of what they called Ruling Elders, and in some other minor details, — which were mainly due to some disproportionate stress laid by them upon certain passages of Scripture, upon which time and experience superinduced a truer exposition, — there were slight differences between them and those churches of the same order which exist to-day. But, in all great essentials, they and their spiritual children are one. The Articles of Faith of Henry Ainsworth's Brownist Church at Amsterdam, in 1596, would need but few words of alteration to make them fit the average needs, and uses, of the Congregational churches of to-day.

The difference between the original Congregationalism of the Massachusetts and the Plymouth colonies seems to have been largely due to the fact, that those who thought out the latter, went to the Bible under the one controlling idea that the Church of England, as then existing, had departed from the Word; and with the one controlling purpose to recover, if possible, the exact primitive and apostolic method; and with no particular bias toward one result rather than another: while the former approached the Bible with the design of expounding its teachings indeed, but with so decided a prejudice against the then so disreputable Separatist or Brownist views, that it was nearly morally certain that their exegesis could, only in the last extremity be driven to that full result. And it was not strange that " the speaking aristocracy in the face of a silent democracy " of Samuel Stone, and Cotton's doctrine of the power of the elders, " with *consent* of the brethren," should have been resorted to by them in the endeavor to avoid an immediate plunge into that absolute democracy, which, both for Church and State, was as much an object of dread in those days in Boston and the towns of the Bay, as it was practically trusted, and found salubrious, in the humbler and older " Old Colony."

That which is simple, natural, and unforced is apt to abide when that which is adroit, and done for a transitory purpose, fails to suit and satisfy the exigencies of the ages. So that it is no strange thing which has happened, that the Congregational churches of New England have gradually worked themselves clear from the aristocratic elements which modified the beginnings of so many of them; ignored, and quietly left to fall into disuse, the Presbyterianish principles which found their way into the Cambridge, and which gave form and force to the Saybrook, platform; and have practically come to their permanent bearings upon the solid, earth-centering rock of democracy, — never better defined than unconsciously in that wonderful compact signed in the cabin of the Mayflower, as a combination into a "body politick for our better ordering, preservation, and furtherance of ye ends [sought therein], and by vertue hearof to enacte, constitute, and frame such just & equall lawes, ordinances, acts, constitutions, & offices, from time to time, as shall be thought most meete & convenient for ye generall good; — unto which we promise all due submission and obedience."

When reduced to its first principles, government must either lodge its power in one ruler, or in all who are ruled, or — between these extremes — in a ruling class; and so it must be essentially either monarchy, or democracy, or aristocracy. Congregationalism is democracy applied to church affairs. It holds Christ to be supreme, and under him it vests ecclesiastical power in the associated brotherhood of local churches; which are bound to maintain a family relation of fraternity and counsel, yet which are in themselves self-complete and independent.

These three systems of polity — the democracy of Congregationalism, the aristocracy of Presbyterianism, and the monarchy of Episcopacy * — are scarcely sufficiently alike, either in principles or processes, to run much risk of being confounded with each other; so that, if the New Testament says

---

* " The Hartford Churchman " of 22d May, 1869, contains an elaborate argument designed to prove, that, so far from being a monarchic government, Episcopacy more nearly represents the democracy of our Republic than any other polity. And this because the Governor of the Commonwealth and the Bishop of a diocese are both " chosen by the votes of their peers." But the essential feature of monarchy is in the fact, that, however elected, the monarch rules; and the essential feature of republicanism is, that, through their elected officers, the people rule. And it requires but the slightest acquaintance with the facts to settle it, on this rule, that Episcopacy is not republicanism, whatever else it may be; and that Congregationalism is republicanism itself, in religion.

any thing at all about church polity, either in the way of describing such of its activities as make themselves matters of its history, or of laying down any precepts whatsoever with regard to it, it would seem to be quite a thing impossible that the careful student of it should be left in doubt whether the churches which the apostles founded, and to whom the Epistles were addressed, were, in the main and characteristically, Congregational, Presbyterian, or Episcopal churches.

We undertake an examination of the New Testament with this inquiry in mind. We mean to glance at every passage in it which casually, or carefully, refers in any manner to church action and government. And, if we have not been wholly misled in our investigations of the Word, we shall be conducted, by such an examination, to the conclusion that the Congregational polity of our Pilgrim Fathers, which they reverently deduced from it, is the polity of the New Testament.

CHAPTER I.

CONGREGATIONALISM IN THE GOSPELS.

Now, then, we approach the question, what kind of church life and action, as a matter of fact, is to be found suggested in the way of precept, and recorded in the way of practice, in the New Testament? Did Christ, so far as he prompted any form of church-life, prepare the minds of his apostles for the democratic, the aristocratic, or the monarchic polity? And were those earliest churches, whose history, with more or less of detail, it gives or hints, characterized by the essential peculiarities of the Congregational, Presbyterian, or Episcopal systems? That is the question, — one would think susceptible of easy and unerring answer.

That answer, it is fair to say here, is rendered less obvious, however, to the merely English reader of the New Testament than it need be in a perfectly accurate translation; than it would have been if King James's translators had not sometimes modified earlier versions in the interest of Episcopacy, nor sometimes, without crowding the sense harder than it will honestly bear, in the direction of prelacy.*

We propose in this chapter a rapid glance at all those passages in the four Gospels which make reference, either in the way of

* The translation by them of the word πάσχα (*passover*) by "Easter" (Acts xii: 4); of the word ἐπισκοπὴν (*office*) by "bishoprick" (Acts i: 20); of the word ἐπισκόπους by "bishop" in several passages of the Epistles, when they had rendered it simply " overseers " in Acts xx: 28; of as many as seven different Greek words (διατασσω, 1 Cor. vii: 17; καθὶστημι, Tit. i: 5, Heb. viii: 3; κρινω, Acts xvi: 4; ποιεω, Mark iii: 14; τασσω, Rom. xiii: 1; τίθημι, 1 Tim. ii: 7; and χειροτονεω, Acts xiv: 23), neither one of which properly signifies what general readers naturally understand by the term, by the phrase " ordain," — are examples of what is here meant. So Acts xiv: 23 retained in the English versions, until the hand of Episcopal authority struck it out, the recognition of the action of the membership of the churches in the choice of their elders. Tyndale (1534) reads, "And when they had ordened them Elders *by eleccion* in every congregation." Cranmer (1539) reads, " And when they had ordened them elders *by eleccion* in every congregacion." The Genevan (1557), " And when they had ordeined them elders *by election* in every church." The authorized version (1611) struck out this reference to the people, and made the act that of the apostles alone, &c.

precept or example, direct or indirect, near or remote, to the subject of church government; of course, with comment of the most brief and condensed description.

And, in proceeding, it is needful to remember, that our Lord left the work of *finishing* to be done by the apostles, under the superintendence of the Holy Spirit. This was true in the vitalest matters of theology. Jesus planted the seeds, they ripened the fruit. It was necessary for him to die before the great central doctrine of the Atonement could be seen by them in its true aspect, as the propitiation for their sins, and not for theirs only, but also for the sins of the whole world; and before those other doctrines which grow out of it, and depend upon it, could assume their logical place, and take on their relative force. So, also, in the matter of the church, and of church-life, Christ contented himself with making a few suggestions,—commands in spirit but not in form,—and laying down a general principle, with a single rule, leaving it for the apostles to carry them out to their necessary conclusions, while he should guide them in the work of laying church foundations, when the time came for it, by his supervising Spirit. As, moreover, the matter of church form must necessarily be among those things reached, if reached at all, only in the closing stages of his career, we ought to expect to find very few, if any, references to it in the four Gospels.

It so happens that the first word which is reached in the harmonized New Testament, which seems to have any flavor of ecclesiasticism about it, is one (Mark iii: 14) which illustrates the criticism we have made upon King James's translators as sometimes, for substance, corrupting the text in the interest of Episcopacy. They tell us that Jesus " ordained twelve, that they should be with him ; " and so forth.

This, if it were correct, would not mean much, but would sound about as, Episcopally, it ought to sound. The Greek word is $\pi o\iota\acute{e}\omega$ (*poieō*). This is employed four or five hundred times in the New Testament, and always in the sense of either " to make " or " to do," — as it is used to imply action as being completed or continued. *In no other instance* does our common version translate it "ordain." It means here simply "to make to become;" that is, to *appoint*. Tyndale (A.D. 1380) renders it, "And he made that there weren twelue with hym." The Genevan version (A.D. 1557) gives it, "And he appoynted twelue, that they should be with hym." Even the Romanist Rheims version (A.D. 1582) has it, "And he made that tvvelue should be with him." It is curious to notice, also, in this connection, how the authors of the common version elsewhere strained another verb in the same direction. They represent Christ (John xv: 16) as saying to the twelve, "I have chosen you, and *ordained* you, that ye should go and bring forth fruit," and so forth. The Greek word here is τίθημι (*tithēmi*), which means "to set," "to put," and so also "to put to some certain use," and hence "to appoint." It is used ninety-six times in the New Testament, and has always been rendered in one of those senses, or in one directly secondary to them, except here, and in 1 Tim. ii: 7, in both of which they have translated it "ordained;" and this although in 2 Tim. i: 11 precisely the same Greek words are made to read, "Whereunto I am *appointed* a preacher."

We find one class of texts in the Evangelists, from the lips of our Saviour, which inculcates very strongly the general principle of the equal brotherhood of believers. This class is represented by such passages as those (Matt. xviii: 1–14, Mark ix: 33–50, Luke ix: 46–50) where the question who should be greatest was discussed by the disciples, and answered by our Lord's putting a little child in the midst of them and saying, "He that is least among you all, the same shall be great;" by those (such as Matt. xx: 1–16) which declare that even those who come in at the eleventh hour shall receive equal wages, without wrong to those who have borne the heat and burden of the day; by those like that (Matt. xx: 20–28, Mark x: 35–45) which replies to the request of the mother of Zebedee's children, by teaching that the true primacy is that of doing most, rather than of ruling most, or having most; those which (like Matt. xxiii: 1-12) rebuke the assumptions of the Pharisees, and the aristocracy of their spirit; and that (John xiii: 1-20) which pictures the Lord as washing the disciples' feet, to teach them humility and fraternity.

It is not, of course, pretended that there is any direct development here of distinctively Congregational teaching; but only that all this points that way, is more harmonious with it than with its opposites, and is what would be most naturally to be expected, if our Lord had that system in mind, as that into which his Spirit should eventually guide believers. We certainly do maintain, that when Jesus said to his disciples, "The princes of the Gentiles exercise dominion over them, and they that are great exercise authority upon them; but *it shall not be so among you*," etc.; and when he commanded them, "Be not ye called Rabbi, for one is your master, even Christ, *and all ye are brethren;* neither be ye called masters, for one is your master, even Christ," etc., he laid down a theory of social and church life which it is next to impossible to realize, except by the Congregational way.

We next come to the one law which our Saviour did enact on this subject; and we are prepared to maintain that this cannot be kept, in perfect good faith, by any other system of church order than our own. This (Matt. xvii: 15–18) is the permanent statute of church discipline. "Moreover, if thy brother shall trespass against thee, go and tell him his fault between thee and him alone; if he shall hear thee, thou hast gained thy brother. But if he will not hear thee, then take with thee one or two more, that, in the mouth of two or three witnesses, every word may be established. And if he shall neglect to hear them, tell it unto the church; but, if he neglect to hear the church, let him be unto thee as an heathen man and a publican." Here we claim that the telling to the church (1) cannot be done under the Romanist or Episcopal system, because neither the Pope, nor the College of Cardinals, nor any Archbishop or Bench of Bishops, nor General Convention, can be "the church" in the sense demanded here; and the local congregation, which is the only one to whom the telling can be done, is utterly without power to act with regard to it; nor (2) can it be done under the Methodist system, for a like reason; nor (3) under the Presbyterian system, for that their "judicatory" comes in between the individual and the church, and makes it literally impossible for him to obey Christ's command. "The church" (ἐκκλησία — *ekklēsia*) here means the local body of believers with which the party is connected. It cannot mean any thing else. Even Alford (Dean of a High Church) is constrained to testify here, "That *ekklēsia* cannot mean the church, as represented by her rulers, appears by verses 19, 20, where *any* collection of believers is gifted with the power of deciding such cases." And he is honest enough to add, "Nothing could be further from the spirit of our Lord's command than proceedings in what are oddly enough called 'ecclesiastical courts.'" And

Lange says, " The term *ekklēsia* must always be understood as referring to the Christian church, or to the meeting of believers, whether it be large or small. . . . Roman-Catholic interpreters are entirely in error in explaining the passage, 'Tell it to the bishops.' "

That this is the true exposition of the word " church " * here becomes inevitable when we reflect that the very object of friendly labor with the offender by the mass of his neighbor believers, as supplementing the work of the " two or three," and tenderly aiming to quicken and guide his conscience, to persuade him that his accusation is no mere misjudgment on the part of a little knot of interested or prejudiced persons,

---

* The Episcopalian suggestion, that, when this was spoken, there was no church in existence, and Christ must have meant the synagogue, which they insist was a very undemocratic institution, overlooks the fact that Christ was speaking for the future, when churches should exist; while Paul's remark concerning the man who had been excommunicated (2 Cor. ii: 6), "Sufficient to such a man is this punishment, which was inflicted by *the many* " (i.e., the multitude of church members), shows that Christ's rule was democratically applied, under the oversight and with the approval of Paul himself.

but does indeed deserve his gravest reconsideration, and call for his deepest penitence, must necessarily become thwarted by the substitution of any thing resembling the process of a series of appellant tribunals with a remote and distant judgment upon his case; and this to that degree as to be rendered absolutely impossible.

We insist, then, that by enacting, as the permanent law of discipline for offences among his followers, one which can be thoroughly and loyally carried out by the Congregational system, and cannot be so applied by any other, our Saviour did in substance ordain the democratic, as the true polity for his church.

It remains, under this part of our subject, only to notice the fact that the idea of the essential fashion of the future Christian church having been thus substantially decreed by Christ, as we have seen that it had already been hinted in spirit by him, his subsequent important utterances conformed themselves to the same conception. This was especially the fact in (John xvii: 1-26) his last prayer for his followers; in (Matt. xxvi: 26–29; Mark xiv: 22–25; Luke xxii: 19, 20) his formula of institution for the Lord's Supper; and (Matt. xxviii: 18–20; Mark xvi: 15, 16; Luke xxiv: 36, 49; John xx: 21–23) his last command. With genuine and profound respect for the various excellences of our sister denominations, we do yet most earnestly believe, and most respectfully urge, that no polity so fully as ours is able to accord with and promote the spirit of that divine and loving oneness and brotherhood for which the Saviour prayed; while his last command, addressed, not to any hierarch, or bench of bishops, but to the company of his followers, as a fraternity of equal individuals, who are commanded to " go preach," befits our system better than any other: and our churches are the only ones which are able, with verbal accuracy exactly to copy, in the Eucharist, the words and deeds of its first institution, as Inspiration has preserved them " for our learning."

One passage only, of a seeming contrary to all these, remains to be examined. It is that (Matt. xvi: 18) in which Christ says to Simon, "Thou art Peter, and upon this rock I will build my church," etc. At first glance, this does look as if Peter were appointed to some special foundation work for the church above his brethren, and to give some slight color to the Romish claim of the primacy of this apostle, continued — as they allege — by transfer to the Popes of Rome. It is an obscure passage, and has been very variously interpreted. Some, like Augustine, Jerome, and others, have referred the " rock " to Christ himself; but this seems forced. Some, like the majority of the Fathers, with Huss and Luther, have referred it to Peter's confession of faith in Christ's Messiahship; but this seems scarcely warranted by the facts of the case. Some, like Origen, have applied it to Peter as the representative of believers in general; but this is labored and unsatisfactory. Lange explains the expression as generalizing, so to speak, the individual Peter into what might be called the *petrine* characteristic of the church; viz., faithfulness of confession, as first distinctly exhibited by Peter: but this seems wire-drawn and fanciful. It remains frankly to understand it as spoken of Peter himself in his own proper person, but not, in the Popish sense of Baronius and Bellarmine, as investing him with any primacy; nor, with some Romanists, and many Protestants like Bengel and Crusius, of any speciality in Peter's work as an apostle; but simply to understand our Saviour as saying, " Thou art Peter (*a rock*); and upon this rock-quality (this boldness and firmness of character, this solid fitness for service in the difficult work of winning men to the gospel) I will build my church." And this interpretation, while it satisfies the exigences of the sense, is borne out by the fact that Peter was first to preach Christ to both Jews (Acts ii : 14) and (Acts x : 34) Gentiles.*

Reasonably considered, then, this passage

---

* We are happy to have good Episcopal indorsement of our judgment of this text. " The Hartford Churchman " of 22d May, 1869, in a free criticism upon the general view presented in this chapter, was careful to say that it neither had, nor saw the need of having, any controversy with us as to this explanation of this passage concerning Peter and the rock.

in no sense contradicts or modifies those teachings of fraternal equality among his followers, which Christ had before solemnly announced.

So far, then, as the Gospels are concerned, we maintain, that as Jesus was the visible and only head of his church so long as he remained on earth, and besides him there was no superiority and no ruling, but all were brethren, equal in rights, however unequal in their work or their renown; so it was his theory and purpose in regard to the subsequent development of his church for all the ages, himself to remain, though ascended, its invisible yet real and only head, its membership standing permanently on the same broad platform of essential equality and brotherhood, and its offices being offices of service and not of ruling.

CHAPTER II.

CONGREGATIONALISM IN THE ACTS OF THE APOSTLES.

HAVING examined those hints and foreshadowings of church government which are contained in the four Gospels, and the one fundamental law of church discipline in them laid down by Christ himself; and having reached the conclusion that the theory which best harmonizes all, and the only one which offers to that law its normal and complete development, is that he had from the beginning the democratic polity in mind, and intended to prepare the way for its practical establishment, so soon as, after his crucifixion and ascension, the fulness of time for it should come, — it is next in order to proceed to an examination of the Acts of the Apostles, in the endeavor to determine what kind of churches under the guidance of the Holy Ghost, were actually formed by those first laborers, and what were their conditions.

1. And the first passage which we find bearing upon the subject is that giving, in the first chapter (verses 15-26), the account of the choice of an apostle in place of Judas. Here the main points of interest are the facts, that, although Peter was spokesman and leader of the eleven, he assumed no such primacy as would fill the vacant apostolate, nor intimated that the eleven collectively had power to fill it; but submitted the matter to the whole church then present, of one hundred and twenty members, telling them that from those who were competent, "one must be *made*" (not "ordained") "a witnesse of his resurexcioun with us," as Wiclif rightly translated it; that the church then (literally) "selected to stand up as candidates," two; and then, recognizing Christ, who had chosen all of the eleven, to be their still existing, though risen, Master and Head, they prayed him to indicate, by the lot, which of the two he preferred; which resulted in the designation of Matthias. There is no mistaking this. Even Chrysostom says, "Peter did every thing here with the

common consent; nothing by his own will and authority. He left the judgment to the multitude, to secure their respect to the elected, and to free himself from every invidious reflection. He did not himself appoint the two; it was the act of all." * While only the germs of any system are here developed, it is clear that these are essentially democratic in their character.

2. It is next noticeable, that (ii: 1, 3, 4) the gift of the Holy Spirit was not confined to apostles or disciples, but was shared by every member. "*All* were with one accord in one place;" and "it sat upon *each* of them;" and "they were *all* filled with the Holy Ghost." This sounds very little like the language of the Episcopal church, which represents the bishop as laying his hands upon the head of the candidate for the priesthood, saying, "Receive the Holy Ghost," but which has no such word to utter in the ear of its candidates for confirmation, and the Lord's table.

3. The next passage which attracts atten-

* *Hom. ad Act* 1, 25.

tion, as having indirect relation to this question of polity, is that (ii: 44, 45, interpreted by iv: 32, 34) which refers to the social life of the believers in Jerusalem, in the opening stage of the existence of the Christian church. They " were together; " that is, they met in the same place, — which is one radical feature of a Congregational church, in distinction from the Presbyterian or Episcopal theories of a great organic all-embracing church, which, as a church, can never be together, but which can only meet in separate congregations, no one of which is a church by and in itself; and they " held all things as common," which, being compared with and interpreted by the subsequent passage, implies not community of goods, as has often been supposed, but the most democratic sharing of the property which they individually owned with each other.* No one called the things which he possessed his own; that

* " Does this description of a community of goods imply that a *general* custom admitting of no exceptions prevailed, so that every individual (not indeed compelled by a law, but in a voluntary manner) sold all his real estate, and placed the proceeds at the disposal of the church? If, ac-

is, no one retained possession of his property in a selfish, secluding spirit, which allowed others no benefit from it; but, on the contrary, they had all things common, that is, employed all things in such a manner as to supply the wants of all. What we claim here is, that such a record as this connects itself much more naturally with our own, than with any antagonist polity.

4. Next we come (iv; 23-33) to the action of Peter and John, when, for the good deed done to the impotent man, they had been arrested, imprisoned, reprimanded, and dismissed. When thus let go, they went "to their own;" that is, not to the apostles and disciples, but to their own church company:

cording to verse thirty-two, not one declared that any of the things which he possessed was his own, this language unquestionably implies that his proprietorship remained undisturbed (*hoc ipso præsupposilur, proprietatem possessionis non plane fuisse deletem*)." — *Bengel, in loco.*

"This passage can by no means be so interpreted as to lead legitimately to the conclusion that it was the universal custom of the members (voluntarily observed, indeed, but still not neglected in a single case), to surrender the whole amount of their real estate for the benefit of poor members. Indeed, the special case which is now adduced leads to the opposite conclusion." — *Lange (Lechler) in loco.*

for when they had made their report to the church, then they *all* prayed, apparently with one voice as well as one spirit; and, when their prayer was done, they were *all* filled with the Holy Ghost; and (the record runs on without any break) this " mass " (τὸ πλῆθος — *to pléthos*) of believers had one heart and one soul, and great grace was upon them *all;* that is, as Lange (Lechler) says, " not on the apostles only, but on all the believers." This procedure was wholly natural, if substantial Congregationalism was their type of church-life; wholly unnatural, if not almost incredible, on any other supposition.

5. The choice of the seven helpers (vi: 1-6) next claims our consideration. Difficulty arose between the Hellenist and the Hebrew portions of the church, because of what the former thought an unequal distribution of the daily dole; whereupon the twelve called together (τὸ πλῆθος — *to pléthos*) the mass of the church, stated the case to them, and told them (1) what they did not desire, — to leave preaching to serve tables; (2) what they did desire, — to continue to

minister the word; with the outgrowing proposition to the church to choose seven fit men to attend to the secularities. This proposition pleased the ($τὸ$ $πλῆθος$ — *to plēthos*) mass of the church; and it selected out Stephen and his six associates, and presented them to the apostles, who set them apart to their work by prayer, and the laying their hands upon them. This, taken in all its parts, was a thoroughly Congregational procedure; radically such, and irreconcilable with any other than the democratic form of church government.

6. What took place on occasion of the first persecution (viii: 1–4) is next in order. It immediately followed the martyrdom of Stephen; and the result of it was to banish to the surrounding regions of Judæa, and to Samaria, even as far as to Phœnicia, and Cyprus, and Antioch, the great majority of the members of the Church at Jerusalem, with the exception of the apostles. But it is expressly said that these fleeing believers " went everywhere preaching the word." These were private Christians, every

one; clothed with no ecclesiastical function, and invested only with that general priesthood which Congregationalism, in accordance with the word (1 Pet. ii: 5–9), assigns to all believers; and yet the term here used to designate the manner of that labor is precisely that ($εὐαγγελίζω$ — *euanggelizō*) which, twenty-two verses after, describes the preaching of Peter and John in Samaria; which Paul employed (1 Cor. i: 17) to announce his special function of preaching the gospel; and which he uses nearly twenty times in the Epistles, in that connection. Nor is this all. In the second reference to the same thing (xi: 19, 20), the idea is repeated in another form; a synonyme being used ($λαλέω$ — *laleō*), which is afterward more than once employed to designate the preaching of Paul and Barnabas, as it had been before used (Mark ii: 2), of the preaching of Christ himself. Thus " the preaching of Jesus to the Greeks in Antioch and elsewhere," says Lange, " was effected not by Peter, nor by any other apostle, but by ordinary Christians and church-members." If these were all substantially Congregationalists, this is a perfectly natural record; if they were any thing else, it becomes not merely abnormal, but surprising.

7. The circumstances connected with Paul's first visit to Jerusalem after his conversion next (ix: 26, 30) invite a glance. When Paul reached that city, he did not report himself to any primate in command, but sought to join himself unto the body of believers; but they, knowing what he had been of old, and seeming to fear that his alleged conversion might be a feint, were suspicious of him, and drew back, until Barnabas — a neighbor by birth, and who seems to have had a previous acquaintance with him, awakening confidence — indorsed him to the apostles; as the result of which, all seem to have been satisfied. And yet it was " the brethren," and not the apostles, which " sent him forth " to Tarsus.

8. The next succeeding verse (ix: 31). offers one of those bits of indirect testimony which lawyers so much value. " Then," that is after the persecution which arose about

Stephen had subsided, " had *the churches* rest throughout all Judea and Galilee and Samaria," etc. This was exactly what would be said if the principles of Congregationalism were then recognized and dominant; it was precisely what would be unnatural, and indeed impossible, in any other state of things. Congregationally, every one of these local assemblies of believers in those three provinces of Palestine was a church, each as fully and truly so as any; and, in making reference to them, they would be so spoken of, as, in fact they always were; as witness chapters xiii: 1, xv: 4, xviii: 22, and xx: 17. But, by the Presbyterian or the Episcopal theory, these were only separate branches of the ONE CHURCH, and must have been in that way described. This manner of speaking is, moreover, uniform. Paul (xv: 41) went from Antioch after the contention between him and Barnabas, "through Syria and Cilicia, confirming *the churches;*" and as the result of his labors, with those of Silas [xvi: 5], were "*the churches* established in the faith." So obvious is the Congregationalism of this manner of record, that the Roman-Catholic authors of the Rheims version (A.D. 1582) seem to have thought it important to mis-translate the first of these texts, and rendered it, " THE CHVRCH truely through al Ievvrie and Galilee and Samaria had peace," etc. But even they did not venture to tamper with the other two.

9. A circumstance connected with the preaching of Peter at the house of the pagan Cornelius at Cesarea (x : 48) should not be overlooked. This centurion sends for the apostle to come from Joppa, gathers together his kindred and friends to hear him, and, in this very hearing, he and they so cordially welcome the truth by faith that the Holy Spirit at once, and with Pentecostal signs, was granted them, — the only instance where it preceded baptism ; clearly to remove every scruple as to an act then so novel as the reception of pagans to the Christian church. Whereupon Peter, assuming that no man could forbid the baptism with water of those who had been already baptized by the Spirit, " gave directions (προστάσσω — *pros-tassō*, ' to

arrange at a place ') that they should be baptized in the name of the Lord." What leans towards Congregational principles, and away from all hierarchal notions, here, is that Peter, who is the only "authorized" official named as being there, did not baptize these people himself, but left it to be done by some of the unofficial Christians who were present (apparently of the "certain brethren from Joppa," who had accompanied him); and that the fact was considered of importance enough to be set down.

10. The controversy at Jerusalem which followed this baptism of Gentiles (xi : 1-18) next claims our notice. What took place at Cesarea was soon heard of at the holy city, and excited attention there; and, when Peter next went there, it led to discussion. Even the primitive churches, being composed of imperfect men, were themselves imperfect; and it was not strange, that, in the welding of the new Christian upon the old Mosaic dispensation, some who had been zealous Jews should unduly cling to Judaism, even to the formation of a party " of the

circumcision " in the church at Jerusalem. This party were dissatisfied with Peter's report of what he had done, and contended with him for so disregarding the old Mosaic law as to eat with uncircumcised heathen. Justice to them requires the remark, that it does not seem to have troubled them that Peter had evangelized Gentiles, but only that he had not first Judaized them by circumcision, before Christianizing them by baptism. Peter replied by a frank statement of the way in which his own scruples had been removed by his vision at Joppa, and by the descent of the Holy Spirit at Cesarea. This quieted all opposition, not merely, but excited the whole church to praise God that the gospel door of hope had been opened to the heathen, as well as to the Jews. Here, now, is no symptom of hierarchy, but every token of democratic brotherhood, and even of apostolic accountability to the associated body of believers.*

---

* " The Hartford Churchman " says on this statement of ours, " As the ' primitive churches ' were ' composed of imperfect men,' they, in a very Congregational way, took exception

11. Next we have (xi : 22) the sending of Barnabas to Antioch, on receipt at Jerusalem of the tidings of the great religious awakening which was taking place at this Greek and Roman capital of Syria, as a consequence of the labors of lay Christians there. This sending was done, not by the bishop, nor by the apostles, but by (ἐκκλησία — *ekklēsia*) the whole church ; another sample of the working of pure primitive Congregationalism.

12. Next in the same chapter (xi : 29) we find the record of the action of these Antiochean believers when the " great dearth " took place subsequently in Judea. Then, not the bishop nor the apostles, not even the elders, moved in the matter ; but " the disciples, every man according to his ability, sent

at St. Peter's conduct in the matter of Cornelius; but we cannot quite agree that this act of the Judaizers is held up as a model to us." Our grateful acknowledgments are due for this concession as to the non-Episcopal facts of this case; and we only need add, that what we are especially searching for now is the fact of the kind of polity actually existing in apostolic times. That being settled, we are willing to leave all concerned to draw their own inferences as to how far what they did was intended to be " a model to us. "

somewhat for aid:" and they sent it "unto the brethren;" although Barnabas and Saul placed it in the hands of "the elders," as it was perfectly natural and Congregational for them to do.

13. Next we come (xiii: 1-3) to the commission of Barnabas and Saul as foreign missionaries by the church at Antioch. To that church, while assembled with worship and fasting, the Holy Spirit said, "Set apart for me Barnabas and Saul, to the work to which I have called them." Then they fasted and prayed, and laid their hands on them, and sent them off. Here the Holy Spirit spake to the body of believers, not to any bishop or primate; and the body obeyed and acted. The command, says Lange, "is not addressed solely to the teachers, but rather to the whole congregation;" and "the immediate consecration and dismission of the two men demonstrate that *the congregation* had clearly understood the revelation of the Spirit. *The believers* laid their hands on both, commended them to God, and sent them forth."

Congruous with this, and precisely responsive to it, was the procedure of these men on their return from this mission. When, after their journeys, trials, and successes (xiv : 27), they came back to Antioch, no mention is made of any statement to any hierarch; but we are told they called together *the whole multitude of the church*, and (ἀναγγέλλω — *anangellō*, " to report back ") gave them an account of what they had done, and of what had been done by their means. Could any thing be more purely consistent with the Congregational way; more inconsistent with any other?

15. The next chapter (xv : 1–31) describes the consultation at Jerusalem. It was the old question of Judaism up again at Antioch; and that church, to reach some safe decision upon it, sent up delegates — " Paul and Barnabas, and certain others " — to lay the subject before the mother-church. When they arrived, they were welcomed by the church and by the apostles and elders; and, in " a congregational meeting " (*Lange*), made a full report of their

work among the Gentiles. Then certain Judeo-Pharisaic members objected against this influx of uncircumcised heathen into the Christian church, and on that objection they seem to have adjourned. Another similar meeting was held (*Lange* says, "Luke speaks only of the apostles and elders; but it distinctly appears, from verses 12, 22, etc., that the congregation was also present, not merely for the purpose of listening, but also of co-operating in deciding the question ") as the result of which, " it pleased the apostles and elders, *with the whole church,*" to send delegates to Antioch, bearing a letter of advice. That letter of advice began by recognizing the church as co-ordinate in power with the apostles, and gave the advice expressly as having " seemed good unto us being assembled (ὁμοθυμαδόν — *homothumadon,* " all together,") that is, by unanimous vote (so *Lange, Bengel, Stier,* and *Meyer*). The bearers of the letter went to Antioch; but they gathered the church together before they delivered (to them) that epistle. And, after these messengers had made their visit, they were sent back to Jerusalem in peace from " the brethren."

It would be difficult to conceive of procedures more laboriously calculated to emphasize the essential principles of Congregationalism, than these taking place under the eye of the apostles, and in the very presence, and with the active co-operation, of that James who is claimed to have been the first primate of Jerusalem.

16. The letter of commendation (xviii: 27) which Apollos carried from the church at Ephesus to that at Corinth, was a Congregational one, given, not by the Bishop, but by the brethren.

17. Paul's sending from Miletus to the elders of the church at Ephesus (xx: 17) was a Congregational procedure. It would be impossible for the whole church at Ephesus to take the journey of some thirty miles to meet him, so he sent (as we should say) for their pastors and deacons, — their chief men; and they responded to his call. If Paul had been an Episcopalian, or a Methodist, or a Presbyterian, he would have

used different language, and have sent for somebody else.

18. And his address to them (xx: 28) was in the spirit of our system too. These men were elders, that is pastors, etc., of the church at Ephesus. He sent for them under that name. Yet now he calls them "bishops," — showing that the only sense which he put upon that word was the Congregational, and not the hierarchal one. "Take heed," he says, " to yourselves, and to all the flock in which the Holy Ghost has set you as (*Episkopous*) BISHOPS"! What a strange High Churchman Paul was, to call these men " bishops"! — half a score (more or less) of bishops in one local church! Even Episcopalian Dean Alford says, " The English version has hardly dealt fairly in this case with the sacred text, in rendering *Episkopous* ' overseers,' whereas it ought there, as in all other places, to have been ' bishops,' that the facts of *elders and bishops having been originally and apostolically synonymous* might be apparent to the ordinary English reader, which now it is not."

19. The little incidental allusions on the journey to Jerusalem, the record of which follows, are alike surcharged with Congregational likelihoods. Paul was "brought on his way" (xxi: 5), not by any bishop or potentate, but by "all;" he "saluted" (xxi: 7) not the bishop of Ptolemais, but "the brethren;" when, with his companions, he reached Jerusalem (xxi: 17), it was not the bishop, nor the rector, but "the brethren," who received him gladly; and at Jerusalem he reported not to James as primate, but (xxi: 18) to him with "all the elders;" and "*they* glorified the Lord," and immediately proceeded to make arrangements for subsequent action, when "the multitude" should come together.

20. And so the faint traces of church order and life which show themselves, as, from this point the narrative sweeps into a swifter current of personal Pauline history, are of the same description to the end. They "found brethren" (xxviii: 14), not a hierarch, at Puteoli; and (xxviii: 15) "the

brethren" came as far as Appii Forum and Tres Tabernæ to meet them.

But these twenty instances are all on one side. Is there absolutely nothing on the other? Yes: we have found exactly five texts in the Book of the Acts, which, unexplained, have a hierarchal look; and these we will now consider.

1. We learn (viii: 14) that the apostles *sent* Peter and John unto Samaria to labor. But this, in terms, is fatal to the Romanists' assumption of Peter's primacy; and there is no evidence that the act was in any sense an ecclesiastical one, or any thing other than might naturally have been looked for as the result of their mutual consultations, as to the best way of fulfilling the Lord's last command.

2. There is a little sound of Episcopacy (xii: 4) in our version's saying "intending, after *Easter*, to bring him forth to the people." But this is a mistranslation. The Greek is *pascha*, which means "the Passover;" and not only Wiclif, but even the Rheims version, so renders it: "meaning after *the Pasche* to bring him forth."

3. A much stronger passage (xvi: 4) is that which makes it appear that Paul and Silas, in their second tour among the churches of Asia Minor, " delivered to them the decrees for to keep, that were ordained of the apostles and elders which were at Jerusalem." But here, if not positive mistranslation, is a distortion of the meaning, in the direction of a hierarchy. The reference is simply to the course of conduct which the previous chapter shows had been agreed upon unanimously by the apostles, elders, and *whole church* at Jerusalem. The word translated decrees (*dogmata*) means also " advice ; " * and such here it was. Wiclif hit the meaning exactly when he translated it, " Gave them to keep *the teachings that were judged* of the apostles and elder men that were at Jerusalem."

4. In like manner the remark of James, which in our version sounds very like that of a bishop (xv: 19), " Wherefore *my sen-*

---

* The Greek noun δόγμα (*dogma*) is derived from the verb δοκεω (*dokeó*) to think. Hence the primary meaning of δόγμα is " that which seems true to one."

tence is," Wiclif reads, " Of which thing I judge;" as also even the Romanist Rheims version: " For the which cause I judge;" the real sense being simply this: " Wherefore my opinion is," * — which makes it a truly Congregational utterance from him.†

5. The only remaining passage, and the only one really deserving of the slightest serious consideration, or demanding any special carefulness of exposition for its correct understanding, is that (xiv: 23) which seems to say of Paul and Barnabas, on the first missionary journey, as they passed through Asia Minor, that " they had ordained them elders in every church." But, whatever the passage does mean, it *cannot* mean that. Nothing is said about " ordina-

---

* " Ἐγὼ κρίνω, — I, for my part, without dictating to others, *judge*, i.e., decide as my opinion." — *Hackett, in loco.*

† " The *Churchman's* comment on this is, " The 'dogmata' *had* the force of decrees, and *were* something more than 'advisory.' " If any proof of this assertion had occurred to it, we may rest assured it would have been produced; and we are therefore grateful for this concession that there exists no better evidence of the Episcopacy of this transaction, than the emphatic opinion of an Episcopalian living eighteen centuries after!

tion" in the Greek. It is declared that Paul and Barnabas (χειροτονήσαντες — *cheirotonēsantes*, which means " to choose by voting with the hand," and hence, " to elect or appoint in any way,") either themselves elected, or superintended the election by each church, of elders. Lange explains it thus: " The expression suggests the thought that the apostles may have appointed and superintended a congregational election." Tyndale translated it, "And when they had ordened them elders by eleccion in every congregacion." Cranmer (A.D. 1539) and the Geneva version render it in the same way. But King James's translators, in the interest of Episcopacy, left out the vital words, " by election." If, now, we read it as they did, we put a hierarchal sense upon the sentence which is not honest, and we throw the verse out of all natural connection with the system of church affairs then prevailing — if we take the testimony of the entire remainder of the Acts of the Apostles. If we even read it "appointed" elders, we commit Paul and Barnabas to a course nowhere else hinted at. But if we read it "*superintended the election of elders* in every church," we treat the verb fairly as to its etymology and history, and we translate the text into symmetry with the entire spirit of the book in which it has its place. Surely, then, no reasonable exegete can fail to reach the result that we have nothing here exceptional to what we have seen to be the unvarying testimony of the book.

There is, then, for there can be, but one conclusion. The system of church polity existing in the beginning, and manifesting itself through the Acts of the Apostles, was essential Congregationalism.* Not yet fully

---

* The *Churchman* says, "The whole argument of 'The Congregationalist' amounts to just this: that the apostles, whom our Lord commissioned and sent, were without power to do any thing but advise; that they had no sooner set about their work, than it was taken out of their hands by the lay members whom they had just converted; and that they never presumed afterwards to interfere or direct. . . . Such a theory will not hold water for five seconds." Begging the *Churchman's* pardon, and, not being immersionists, caring very little about the relations of our argument to water, we beg to insist, that what we gather from the New Testament is, that the apostles were divinely commissioned to act towards the young churches which they founded, precisely as a wise parent

developed, its germs were those of ecclesiastical democracy, in sharp, continual, and irreconcilable hostility with spiritual aristocracy or monarchy.

acts towards his children, — not keep them under authority permanently, but train them by authority, oversight, advice, and every possible influence of affection, to become, as soon as possible, competent to the assumption (under God) of the entire responsibility of their own affairs.

CHAPTER III.

CONGREGATIONALISM IN THE EPISTLES.

Having seen how the foundations of our democratic polity were laid in the teachings of Christ himself, as recorded in the Gospels, and the structure elaborated by the apostles under the supervision of the Holy Ghost, we are now prepared to inquire, in conclusion, what light, incidental or direct, is thrown upon the subject in the various Epistles.

We find it most convenient to classify the testimonies of the Epistles on this subject under the following heads, which include them all; viz., (1) texts which refer to a church, or to churches, in a way scarcely explicable except on the Congregational theory; (2) those which clearly contemplate and advise such a brotherhood as can exist in its fulness only in the Congregational way; (3) those which seem to be founded upon the supposition that the churches were of a democratic character; (4) those which speak of church officers in a manner natural only to Congregationalism; (5) those which require or refer to church action possible only to our polity; and (6) those which seem to suggest another system, but which, when justly explained, are really corroborative of all the rest in suggesting ours.

1. The use which is habitually made of the word ἐκκλησία (*ekklēsia*) in the singular and plural, is such as is consistent only with the Congregational doctrine of the church. In more than fifty instances in the Epistles, the term is used under circumstances clearly implying a single congregation of believers. The churches at Cenchrea, Corinth, Philippi, Laodicea, Thessalonica, in the house of Priscilla and Aquila, in the house of Nymphas, and in the house of Philemon, are specifically named, and one is implied at Hierapolis; besides the general mention of the churches "of the Gentiles," "of Christ," "of God," "of Galatia," "of Asia," "of Macedonia," and "in Judæa;" besides more indefinite allusions to "the churches," and "all

churches:" and in the Apocalypse we read of the church at Ephesus, at Smyrna, at Pergamos, at Thyatira, at Sardis, at Philadelphia, and at Laodicea; while these are grouped, and written of collectively, as " the seven churches of Asia." On a careful examination, moreover, it becomes obvious, that, beyond question, some of these churches were so near that they might readily have been fused into one, if it had not been thought expedient to include in a single church only those believers who could regularly and conveniently unite in the enjoyment of its privileges, and the performance of its duties. For example, Cenchrea was the suburb and port of Corinth; yet there were churches at both places. Hierapolis was visible from the theatre of Laodicea, and Colosse was near, some think directly between, them; while Nymphas appears to have lived in or near Laodicea, and it is almost certain that Philemon was a resident of Colosse. So that there is the strongest probability that these five churches — at Hierapolis, Laodicea, Colosse, and in the houses of Nymphas and Philemon — were all situated within a very short distance, probably within sight of each other; — near enough, at least, to demonstrate, by the fact of their individual existence, that it was the aim of the apostles to include within a given *ekklēsia*, only those members who could well and habitually share its privileges, and carry on its labors. This is not only Congregationalism, but this employment of the term "church" is inconsistent with any other polity. "Its use," says the late Dr. Vaughan, "as signifying the ministers of religion in distinction from the people, or as embracing all the persons professing Christianity in a province or nation, is unknown to the Sacred Scriptures. We read in the New Testament of 'the church at Jerusalem,' the 'church in the house of Priscilla and Aquila,' and of 'the churches in Judæa, Galatia,' etc.; but we meet with no such phrase as 'the church of Judea,' or 'the church of Galatia.' This application of the term was reserved until the time when Christianity became established as a part and parcel of the kingdoms of this world."

2. We find in the Epistles a large number of texts which obviously contemplate, and seek to further, precisely such a spirit of equal brotherhood and co-working, and such mutual responsibility, as are peculiar to Congregationalism. Thrice repeated by Paul to three different churches (Rom. xii: 1-8; 1 Cor. xii: 1-31; Eph. iv: 4-16), was the general symbol of a church as a body with many members, having not the same office nor the same gifts; but yet with none less honorable than others, or less essential to the general work: so that the whole body, thus made up of fraternal parts, maketh increase by that which every joint supplieth. So also he commands every Roman believer (Rom. xv: 2) to "please his neighbor, for good ends, to build him up." [In the Pauline Epistles, where the sense seems to be improved thereby, we make use of the Conybeare and Howson translation, against which Episcopalians surely ought not to object.] He is persuaded (xv: 14), that they are able

" of [yourselves] to admonish one another;" he exhorts " the brethren " (xvi: 17) to keep their eyes upon " those who cause divisions, and cast stumbling-blocks in the way of others, contrary to the teaching which [they] have learned." So he exhorts the Corinthian " brethren " (1 Cor. i: 10) " to shun disputes, and have no divisions, but to be knit together in the same mind and the same judgment." It is the only blemish which he suggests as existing in the church at Philippi, that certain of its members were deficient in lowliness of mind, and were thus led into disputes and altercations with their brethren; and so he says (ii: 2–4), " Be of one accord, filled with the same love, of one soul, of one mind. Do nothing in a spirit of intrigue or vanity; but, in lowliness of mind, let each account others above himself. Seek not your private ends alone; but let every man seek likewise his neighbor's good."

He beseeches " the holy and faithful brethren" at Colosse (Coloss. iii: 16) to " teach and admonish one another, in all wisdom." Peter told the Christians of the churches of Asia (1 Pet. ii : 9, 10) that they, having been chosen out of the world, were a royal priesthood, a separated and holy people, a purchased company, to the end that they should publish abroad the virtues and perfections of God and Christ; and (iii : 8) he finally exhorts them to be especially mindful of their fraternity of spirit. Paul told the " brethren " of the churches of Galatia (Gal. vi : 2) to " bear one another's burdens, and so fulfil the law of Christ; for if any man exalts himself, thinking to be something when he is nothing, he deceives himself with vain imaginations;" and he admonished the Hebrews (xiii : 1) to " let brotherly love continue;" he informed the Romans (xv : 25, 26, 31) that the brethren of Macedonia and Achaia had " willingly undertaken to make a certain contribution for the poor among the saints in Jerusalem; " and he asked their prayers that his service in carrying this contribution might " be favorably received " by the brethren there. Very touching, also, is the declaration of John (1 John v : 16), — which implies the lodgement of responsibility for those church-members who wander, not in any functionary, but in the body of the brotherhood, — that if any brother "see his brother sinning a sin not unto death (that is, one which does not absolutely annul fellowship with Christ, and cut off faith in him), he shall ask, and gain for him life," etc.

3. There is a class of passages in the Epistles which seems tacitly to assume that the state of things was what it would naturally be, only if these apostolic churches then existing were Congregational ones. Among these are the first, the salutatory, verses of almost every Epistle. They are not addressed to the primates of the churches under any name, but almost always to the brotherhoods themselves, precisely as Congregational letters-missive are now addressed. That to the Romans is "to all God's beloved, called to be Christians, who dwell in Rome;" the first to the Corinthians, "to the Church of God at Corinth;" the second, "to the Church of God which is in Corinth, and to all Christians throughout the whole Province of Achaia;"

that to the Galatians, "to the churches of Galatia;" that to the Ephesians (or, as many hold, the Laodiceans), "to the Christians who are at Ephesus" [Laodicea]; that to the Colossians, "to the holy and faithful brethren in Christ who are at Colosse;" those to the Thessalonians, "to the Church of the Thessalonians." The others were either more general in their scope, like that to the Hebrews, which is rather a treatise than an Epistle, and was addressed to the class of Christianized Hebrews as such, rather than to the churches of which they were members; and Peter's, which was a general letter to all who had "obtained like precious faith:" or more specific, like Paul's to Timothy, Titus, and Philemon, — with the single exception of that to the Philippians, which is addressed "to all Christians in Christ Jesus who are at Philippi, *with the bishops and deacons.*" * The reason of this addition does

* "It is singular that the presbyters and deacons should be mentioned separately in the address of this Epistle only. It has been suggested that they had collected and forwarded the contribution sent by Epaphroditus." — *Conybeare and Howson,* in loco.

not appear; but it does appear that this could not have been an Episcopal church at Philippi, or it would have had but one bishop; and also that the church ranked in Paul's eyes before its officers.

So Peter appeals to "*the brethren,*" and seeks (2 Pet. iii: 1) "to stir up [their] pure minds by way of remembrance," when he desires to forefend the cause from the danger of scoffers; and it is the " brethren " whom he is addressing when he says (1 Pet. iv: 11), " If any speak, let him speak as the oracles of God; if any minister, let him do it as of the power which God bestoweth." It is the hierarchal claim that Timothy was a bishop; but Paul tells him (1 Tim. iv: 6) that "if he puts *the brethren* in remembrance of these things " (that is, the confutation of various errorists which he has just been indicating), "he will be a good servant of Jesus Christ."

So what Paul says to the Thessalonian church (1 Thess. v: 12), in regard to the treatment which he desires them to give their elders, or pastors, is precisely what would have been natural on the Congregational, and to the last degree unnatural on any other, theory. " I beseech you, brethren, to have due sympathy with those who are laboring among you; who preside over you in the Lord's name, and keep you in mind of your duty. I beseech you to esteem them very exceedingly in love, for their work's sake." Quite akin in spirit to this is what the same apostle said to the Hebrews (xiii: 17), " Render unto them that are your leaders obedience and submission; for they, on their part, watch for the good of your souls, as those that must give account: that they may keep their watch with joy, and not with lamentation; for that would be unprofitable for you."

We do not claim that these passages can, of themselves, establish the doctrine of the democracy of the primitive churches; only that they best comport with it, and furnish collateral evidence of weight, when that democracy has been otherwise reasonably proved.

4. The more direct references to the

officers of these churches establish the Congregationalism of these bodies. There are only two orders of church-officers spoken of in the Epistles; viz.: (1) those who are indiscriminately called pastors (in the Apocalypse "angels"), teachers, presbyters (or elders), and bishops (or overseers); (2) deacons. That the first four names were different designations of the same office appears, first, from the fact that the same persons are called (Eph. iv: 11) pastors *and* teachers; that the elders are (as 1 Tim. v: 17) spoken of as the only officers besides deacons which the churches had, and hence must be the same as those elsewhere called pastors or teachers; and that Paul (Acts xx: 28) expressly told the "elders" of the church at Ephesus that the Holy Ghost had made them "bishops" of that flock: while Paul to Titus (i: 7) says the "*elders*" must be blameless, for the reason that "a *bishop* ought to be blameless," etc.; showing that he had the same persons in mind. Then, in the second place, precisely the same qualifications (1 Tim. iii: 2–7; Tit. i: 6–10) are demanded of pastors, teachers, elders, and bishops. In the third place, the same duties are assigned to all : (1) to guide the church by counsel and authority (1 Tim. v : 17 ; Acts xx : 28) ; (2) to instruct the church (1 Tim. iii : 5 ; Tit. i : 9). And, in the fourth place, the fact that there is not a passage in the New Testament which asserts, or justifies the assertion of, any superior function on the part of the bishops, completes the proof that only two orders of officers were known to the churches of the New Testament, and that these were the pastors (elders, presbyters, bishops) and deacons of the Congregational churches of the present. Even Peter, who was, if Romanists are right, the very chiefest of the Apostles, says (1 Pet. v : 1), " The elders which are among you I exhort, *who am also an elder.*" Lange (Fronmüller) says on this passage, " After the apostolic age, the offices of bishop and elders were gradually separated. During the life-time of the apostles, the supreme direction of the churches was wielded by them; but they put themselves on a level with the elders." *

One passage in this connection has given unauthorized comfort to our Presbyterian friends (1 Tim. v: 17): "Let the elders that rule well be counted worthy of double honor, especially they who labor in the word and doctrine." But there is no *lay-eldership* here. Lange says, "No footsteps are to be found in any New-Testament church of lay-elders; nor were there for many hundred years." These were simply associate pastors, some of whom paid special attention to the government of the church, while others were more given to the word and doctrine. And Paul commends those who performed their office well, as being worthy of a twofold honor.†

---

* "These terms are used in the New Testament as equivalent, — the former (ἐπίσκοπος) denoting (as its meaning of overseer implies) the duties, the latter (πρεσβύτερος) the rank, of the office." — *Conybeare and Howson*, chap. xiii.

† Conybeare and Howson translate this verse, "Let the presbyters who perform their offices well be counted worthy of a twofold honor; especially those who labor in speaking and teaching."

"No footsteps are to be found, in any Christian church, of

But this reference to the two classes of pastors and deacons alone, with the assignment to them of precisely those functions which are usual to officers bearing that name in democratic churches, is proof, of the very strongest kind, that the churches to which these Epistles were written were democratic churches; while the absence of all reference to a hierarchy is incidental evidence of the weightiest character that none existed until after the canon was closed, and our New Testament was completed as it stands.

5. But perhaps the most convincing proof of the Congregationalism of the primitive churches which is furnished by the Epistles, is the illustrations which they give of the method of action pursued in those churches, and in connection with them. Paul (2 Cor. viii : 19) says that Titus "had been chosen

lay-elders, nor were there for many hundred years. St. Paul, prescribing Timothy how he should stablish the church, passeth immediately from bishops and ministers of the word and sacraments to deacons, omitting these lay-elders, that are supposed to lie in the midst between them." — *Dr. Washburn,* in *Lange* (*Van Oosterzee*), in loco.

by the churches" (of Macedonia) to accompany him in his journey; and, farther on (v. 23), he calls him and the unnamed brother who was with him, "the messengers of the churches," to the end of transmitting the gift of the Macedonian churches to the church at Jerusalem. This was a purely Congregational procedure; and the attempt of Bishop Coxe, on the late occasion of the consecration of Dr. Huntington, to dignify this last text (which is the simple historic record of the fact that the two members of the Macedonian churches who had been chosen by those churches to carry, with Titus, their fraternal alms to the Corinthians, went as delegates of those churches, and, in so doing, illustrated and honored their Christian profession) into some kind of a prop to the system of Episcopacy, fell but little short of positive absurdity. "The persons are mentioned," says Lange (Kling), "not as sent of the Lord in any sense, but simply as ($\dot{\alpha}\pi o\sigma\tau o\lambda o\iota\ \dot{\epsilon}\varkappa\varkappa\lambda\eta\sigma\iota\tilde{\omega}\nu$ — *apostoloi ekklēsiōn*) messengers of the churches with reference to a single benevolent mission, or journey. It can surely have no reference here to a permanent office, and is used simply as a common noun."

So Paul's hint of the method of Timothy's setting apart to his ministerial work (1 Tim. iv : 14) by " prophecy, with the laying on of the hands of the elders " (πρεσβυτέριου — *presbuteriou* is translated " elders " in the other two places in which it occurs in the New Testament, and it would make the sense clearer so to translate it here) is as precise an account of the way in which the thousands of Congregational ministers now at their work have been set apart, as our language could give. And, in like manner, James's direction (v : 14), " Is any sick among you ? let him call for the elders of the church, and let them pray over him," etc., whether it is to be taken of bodily, or of soul sickness, was a direction to the primitive churches more consonant with the Congregational, than any other polity.

Specially to be noted, however, are the directions in regard to church discipline which the Epistles contain, which agree with what we have seen before to be the law of Christ, and which precisely accord with the Congregational way, but have no congruity with any other. Paul directs Titus (iii: 10) to "put the brethren in mind," among other things, after one and a second admonition, to reject an heretical man. And he directed " the brethren " of the Church of the Thessalonians (2 Thess. iii: 6) "in the name of the Lord Jesus Christ to withdraw [themselves] from every brother who walks disorderly;" and (verses 14, 15), "if any man be disobedient to my written word, to mark that man, and cease from intercourse with him, that he might be brought to shame; but to count him not as an enemy, but admonish him as a brother,"— counsel which fits the Congregational interpretation of Christ's law of church discipline, with absolute exactness.

Moreover, Paul gives the Corinthians explicit instructions in the same line of procedure (1 Cor. v: 4, 5, 13), and directs them, when gathered together in the church assembly in the name of the Lord Jesus, to deliver over to Satan a certain gross offender, " that his spirit may be saved in the day of the Lord Jesus;" and adds, " From amongst yourselves ye shall cast out the evil person." And, in his Second Epistle (ii: 6), he refers back to the same case, and to the church's compliance with his command, and says, " For the offender himself, this punishment, which *has been inflicted on him by the sentence of the majority*" (so Conybeare and Howson),* is sufficient without increasing it." We undertake to say that it is simply impossible for our Episcopalian, Methodist, or Presbyterian brethren to harmonize this act of the majority of the brethren of the church at Corinth — which was exactly the carrying-out of the rule of the eighteenth of Matthew, and which Paul first advised, and then comments on as "sufficient" — with their theories, or practice, of church government.

6. It remains only to glance, in conclusion,

---

* " The πλείονες, by whom the punishment had been inflicted, could not have been the eldership, but the majority of the church at Corinth." — *Lange* (*Kling*), in loco.

at a cluster of two or three texts, which appear to contain some hierarchic leaning, that we may see how entirely, after all, those passages coincide in spirit with all that have been already examined.

One (1 Cor. vii: 17) our version translates, "And so ordain I in all churches." This seems to put Paul into a position of primacy, which he never dreamed of claiming. What he said was, "So (διατάσσομαι — *diatassomai*) in all the churches." "*Diatassomai*" means simply "to put in order," "to arrange."* It is the same verb which he used (1 Cor. xi: 34) to express "The rest will I *set in order* when I come." And it means here simply, "That is the arrangement which I favor, in all the churches." Wyclif renders it, "As I teche in alle chirchis;" and even the Romanist Rheims' translators give it, "As in al churches I teach." Our version distorts the same verb

---

* Lange (Kling) thus amends the translation of the same verb in another place of the same epistle (xvi: 1): "Now, concerning the collection for the saints, as I have given order to (*arranged throughout,* — διέταξα) the churches of Galatia, even so do ye."

with the like impropriety, in another text also (1 Cor. xvi: 1), where Paul is made to say, " As I have *given order* to the churches of Galatia." Its meaning there is the same as here.

Another passage is (1 Cor. xi: 2) where Paul is represented by our version to command, " Keep *the ordinances*, as I delivered them to you; " which has a look of authority, as of a ruling outside of the church. The Greek word here is παραδόσεις — *paradoseis*, which is used thirteen times in the New Testament, and in *every* other instance is translated " traditions; " as " tradition of the elders," Mark vii: 3, etc. The Rheims version renders it here, " As I haue deliuered vnto you, you keepe my precepts." Tyndale, Cranmer, and the Geneva version agree together thus: " Kepe *the ordinaunces*, even as I delyvered them to you."

Still another text is that (Gal. ii: 9) which seems to intimate that " James, Cephas, and John, who seemed to be pillars," gave to Paul and Barnabas the right hand of fellowship to go to the heathen, as they to the circumcision; as if with some showing of superior authority. A careful examination, however, removes any such look. The fact simply was, that, as the result of mutual advisement as to the best disposal of the Evangelic forces at command, it was mutually agreed that Paul and Barnabas should labor among the Gentiles, and James and Peter and John among the Jews; and, as we may colloquially say, " they shook hands on that;" " for the structure of the Greek seems to make the going of the one party to the circumcision, as true and near a sequence of this symbol of fellowship, as the going of the other to the heathen.

A class of passages remains, which, it has been claimed, " recognize an Episcopate as in being, and give directions as to well-known acts;" such, for example, as Paul's direction to Timothy (1 Tim. v: 22) to " lay hands suddenly on no man;" of which the Hartford *Churchman* says, " No wrenching will twist these words into harmony with the Congregational system." We do not doubt the honesty with which this was said; but its ignorance is marvellous and deplorable. It is a part of the duty and privilege of every Congregational bishop to assist, when providentially called to do so, in that ceremony of setting apart to the ministry on behalf of some church, by which ordination is effected now precisely as it was when the like " gift " was given to Timothy himself " by prophecy, with the laying-on of the hands of the presbytery " (iv : 14). And it is his duty, as it was Timothy's, to exercise due deliberation in that act, and not hastily and unadvisedly to assist to place an unworthy man in a worthy place, and so become a " partaker of other men's sins." It is not easy, from a Congregational point of view, to see how such passages as this can be made to require any " wrenching," except it be to make them usable for the support of the Episcopate ; for which purpose one would think they ought to be twisted so far as to make them teach that Timothy was ordained by the hands of *one* bishop, and not of a whole presbytery (equal band) of pastors.

We are very ready to concede that there

are some texts which need for their true understanding, a careful consideration of the peculiar relations of the apostles to the early churches, and which, in the absence of such consideration, may seem susceptible of some slight hierarchal tinge and tendency. Chief among these is that (Tit. i: 5) in which — as our version gives it — Paul says to Titus, " For this cause left I thee in Crete ; that thou *shouldest set in order* the things that are wanting, and ordain elders in every city, as I had appointed thee." The verse, literally translated, reads thus: " For this cause (that thou shouldest further bring into order the things that are wanting in respect to ecclesiastical organization, and especially appoint or secure the appointment of elders in every city, as I had arranged beforehand) left I thee in Crete." Now, our Episcopalian friends insist that nothing can do justice to the intent and substance of this text, but their theory that Paul was a bishop after their pattern, and Titus a bishop of the same kind, and that both lorded it over God's heritage — which Peter forbade ; instead of being ensamples to the flock — which he commanded.

Now, the Congregational theory provides for a special authority, as well as leadership, on the part of the apostles, and so exactly meets all the requisitions of these passages; without flying in the face, in so doing, of all the rest of the New Testament, as the Episcopalian explanation necessarily does. The apostles were missionaries, with an extraordinary training, inspiration, and authority, peculiar to themselves. They did *rule* these feeble primitive churches, just as our modern missionaries have ruled, for a time, the infant churches which they have founded on heathen ground. They did so *ex necessitate rei*, — because that was inevitable under the circumstances; just as the new settler lives in a log-cabin a little while, not because that is his theory of domestic architecture, but because that is the best he can do for the first year; just as the father guides the tottering steps of his first-born in its amazing initial excursions from one side of the room to the other, because that is the best way of teaching it to walk, and not because he proposes to have the child walk in that manner at maturity, and through life. Paul's directions to Timothy and Titus — his converts — are almost precisely such as are natural, and have been frequent, in the history of our own Congregational missionaries of to-day, in almost those same regions. The churches were what we now call mission-churches, and their pastors (elders) were what we now call native pastors.* And, granting all of authority which this theory naturally brings to the explanation of the circumstances of the churches founded by the apostles, we gain apt and

---

* The *ruling* spoken of in the New Testament is a thing understood in the mission-churches of our day (though perhaps not exactly in the ancient form), where pastoral authority is just as needful in the infancy of these churches, as parental authority is in the early years of a family. Among the churches on the Hawaiian Islands, for instance, the missionaries felt it necessary to exercise authority in the native churches for a course of years; and what of authority remained in the year 1863, and was deemed to be still necessary, was then transferred to the associations and presbytery, the former intending to relinquish it to the local churches, as soon as the native pastorate had made advances to render it a safe deposit." — *Dr. Rufus Anderson in " Congregationalist,"* 4 Aug., 1865.

abundant explanation of these, in a sense exceptional, texts, and do no violence to the essential Congregational spirit which saturates and characterizes the New Testament as a whole.

There is one remarkable claim which has been put forth by the Hartford *Churchman*, which seems to deserve a word of notice here. So far as we can understand it, it amounts to this; viz., that large parts of the " other things which Jesus did " — which if they should be written every one, John (xxi : 25) suggested, would fill so many books that the world could not contain them— were *oral directions upon the subject of Episcopacy!* This fulness of *vivâ voce* utterance to the apostles, it thinks, accounts for the little that is put down in the New Testament ; while it urges, that, being from Christ, it is just as imperative as the written word, and deposited its force in the traditions of the Church, which we are bound to receive. To this ingenious theory, it seems to be quite sufficient to reply, that oral utterances in the ears of the apostles, which made them *act* as Congregationalists, — as we have seen in their Acts and Epistles that they did, — must have been Congregational in their tenor; so that if this argument from " tradition " is worth any thing, it goes to support the democratic, and not the hierarchic polity.

This closes our examination. We have passed in review the principal allusions, nearer or more remote, in the Epistles, to the subject of church government, as before in the Gospels and the Acts. We have found that they contain references to the local church and to the churches, which it is difficult to explain unless those bodies then existing were Congregational in form; that they clearly contemplate and advise such a fraternity as can only be germane to Congregationalism; that they, in many places, seem to take for granted the Congregationalism of all churches; that they treat of church officers as Congregationalists only naturally and consistently can do; that they refer to and require church action which only Congregationalists can self-consistently and fully perform; and that the very few which seem to suggest another system do so in appearance only, and are explicable upon a theory which saves their entire force without throwing them athwart the general tenor of the Word.

This, indeed, was what we had every reason to expect. For it would have been surely very strange, if the Gospels had recorded the foundation laid by Christ for a democratic church government, and the Acts of the Apostles had made it clear, that, under the guidance of the Holy Spirit, the apostles and early Christians, in point of fact, had established Congregational churches, and then the practical letters of the same apostles, in the years immediately subsequent, had ignored them, or implied a different and adverse system. It was most natural that it should be as it is, and that the whole New Testament should cast its absolute weight, without even the deduction and drawback of a single irreconcilable counter passage, for the democratic polity, in distinction from, and in opposition to, those aristocratic and monarchic corruptions which came in in subsequent centuries, when the gold became dim, and the most fine gold was changed, and the world first invaded, and then conquered and assimilated, the church.

CHAPTER IV.

CONCLUSION.

The sons, lineal and spiritual, of the Plymouth men — the Congregationalists of the present time in the United States — do, then, distinctly and broadly claim (as they intend and hope, in due charity towards all), that the Pilgrim Church polity is the polity of the New Testament. They do claim to be the nearest and faithfullest representatives of the churches of the time of the apostles.

They claim, that as Jesus Christ was the head of His church so long as He remained on earth, and besides Him there was no superiority and no ruling, but all were equal brethren, so it was His intent to remain, after His ascension, its invisible but real and only ruler; ruling through the influences of His Spirit upon the broad brotherhood, whose offices should be few and simple, and these for service, and not for show and sway.

They claim that the system of church

government which was actually developed under Christ's one law (of discipline) and general oversight, and through the action and (in some cases, when needful) the ruling of the apostles, is proven by the whole tenor of the book of those apostles' Acts to have been essentially and germinantly democratic, in distinction from spiritual aristocracy and monarchy.

They claim that all this, which is inseparably interwoven with the entire texture of the historic portions of the New Testament, finds natural and unanswerable indorsement from its preceptive portions, so that Gospels, Acts, and Epistles, are one in the averment that that democratic polity which is the Congregationalism of to-day, and which the Brownists rescued and revived from the rubbish of the dark ages, was the polity of the times, the events, and the authors, of the New Testament.

And so they believe that the Pilgrim Fathers were entirely right in the views which made them pray for the success of their polity in these terms, — in Gov. Bradford's words: "That the trueth may prevaile, and the churches of God reverte to their *ancient* puritie, and recover THEIR PRIMITIVE ORDER, LIBERTIE, AND BEWTIE."

www.ingramcontent.com/pod-product-compliance
Lightning Source LLC
Chambersburg PA
CBHW020301090426
42735CB00009B/1175